Stillness And Scars

Where Pain Becomes Poetry and Stillness
Brings Clarity

Swapna Rajasekar

Dedication

To my mother and aunt—two fierce, nurturing forces who raised me like divinity, with grit, grace, and boundless love.

To my uncle, whose faith in me never wavered, even when the world did.

To my partner, who showed me the beauty and ache of unconditional love, and taught me how to give selflessly, even in heartbreak.

And to my little sister, my brightest cheerleader, my mirror soul in a younger form—thank you for reminding me how powerful love, laughter, and loyalty can be.

And to my Godfather—who would have been so proud to see this book come to life. I know you're smiling from the heavens, as you always did, watching over me.

This book is a reflection of all that you poured into me.

This book is because of you. This book is for you.

Preface

Stillness and Scars was born in the quiet moments between chaos and clarity — in the silences I once feared and the wounds I tried to hide. These poems are fragments of a journey — through grief and grace, heartbreak and healing, solitude and soul-searching.

Each piece is a reflection of what it means to fall apart and still find your way back, not to who you were, but to who you were always meant to become.

I didn't write this book because I had all the answers. I wrote it because I had questions — about love, about loss, about purpose, and about the courage it takes to live with an open heart in a world that often asks us to close it.

Whether you are navigating your own shadows or learning how to stand in your light, I hope these words feel like a companion. May you find something here that makes you feel seen, held, and just a little less alone.

Thank you for holding space for my truth — and perhaps, in these pages, discovering echoes of your own.

Swapna

Acknowledgements

This book was born from the quiet hours, the deep wounds, and the steady hands that helped me hold both. I owe its existence to the people and forces that shaped my path, healed my heart, and guided me home to myself.

To my mother & family, whose resilience carved the first shape of strength into my bones — thank you for being my earliest teacher of love, sacrifice, and grace. You gave me the wings to dream and the spine to stand tall.

To my Godfather—you may no longer walk this earth, but I feel your presence in every brave step I take. I hope this book makes you proud.

To my partner, who introduced me to the kind of love that doesn't flinch — the kind that stays, softens, and holds. Your presence has been both mirror and medicine.

To my spiritual Guru, my sole guardian — you are the light that cracked open my understanding of life. Thank you for grounding me in truth, for helping me see the rawness of life not as something to be fixed, but fully embraced. Your wisdom brought me back to myself.

To the countless strangers, friends and silent guides who inspired verses through acts of kindness, service, and truth— this book carries echoes of your spirit.

And finally, to every reader — if these words find you in your ache, your becoming, or your return — thank you for walking with me. This book was written for the scarred and the seeking, the strong and the soft.

With all my heart,

Swapna

I Am Named Dreams

I am named dreams, and I stay true to that—
A life that's wild, wounded, and yet, wonderful.
Like a child wishing on a falling star,
I've whispered countless prayers into the void,
Most never answered—
But don't think I haven't noticed the miracles you made
for me.

While my heart shattered into a thousand pieces,
You crafted moments—
The scent of rain-kissed earth,
The ocean's chill against my skin,
The sun's warm embrace—
Each an invisible hug from you.

What I wanted never came to be,
But sometimes,
My wildest imaginations flickered to life
In the most unexpected ways.
Perhaps you were showing me—

Magic arrives when it's least expected.

I'm still trying to understand this paradox, my life.
Quietly, you've led me to people and paths
That guide me inward—
A silent road to self-discovery.
Don't think I didn't notice.

You didn't give me a role model father,
But you gave me a village—
Souls who loved me like their own.
Some left, some stayed,
All shaped me.
Don't think I didn't notice.

You didn't erase the trauma or the pain,
But you handed me every tool I needed
To rise above it.
Don't think I didn't notice.

I hope you grant me the strength
To turn my wounds into wisdom.
Don't think I didn't notice, God.

Who Is to Blame?

Two adults,
Their hearts yearning for each other
With a divine, magnetic pull.
But the children within them—
Still wounded, still spiteful—
Hold the reins.

One child fears abandonment,
Clings to connection like air.
The other hides,
Suppresses emotion
Like it's a storm too dangerous to face.

One believes love is in presence,
The other in promises.
The adults flutter—
Drawn to each other as if stitched at the soul,
Bonded across lifetimes.
Yet the children cry for help.

Who can you blame?

One child retreats,
Folding into silence—
Afraid of what emotions might surface.
The other throws tantrums,
Yearning for comfort,
For assurance never given.

Who can you blame?

Two children in grown-up skin,
Carrying toddler hearts bruised
By the absence of nurturing.
No one taught them how to love,
How to feel,
How to be okay with not being okay.

One suffers aloud,
The other in silence.
Both aching.

Their emotional scars—
Not born of choice,
But left behind by adults
Who never taught them how to heal.

So, tell me—
Who is to blame?

Invisible, Yet Loved

You are quiet for most of the day,
retreating into yourself,
breathing heavier by nightfall.

You long to be left alone,
yet somewhere,
someone thinks of you—constantly.

You reach for smoke to burn your anger away,
and still,
someone out there prays
you breathe deep the clean, healing air.

You wear toughness like a shield,
though your soul is bruised and battered.
Someone, somewhere,
wishes you'd find the courage
to turn it all around.

You believe you are invisible,

a ghost in the noise—
but to someone,
you are a dream,
a heartbeat,
a whispered hope.

They are waiting,
arms wide open,
ready to say—
I got you, baby.

The Playful Drama of Life

Life —
a grand theater of plot twists,
heartaches, fleeting lessons,
and pockets of laughter stitched in between.

At times, it feels impossibly intricate,
woven with threads too delicate to touch.
We cradle our pain like a fragile heirloom,
thinking it defines us.
We narrate our sorrows to another,
then another,
and by the time the fifth soul listens,
the sharpness dulls.
What once was agony softens into memory,
pain morphs into story,
emotions condense into wisdom,
and decisions become mere jokes told over coffee.

Life is mischievous —
it wraps its seriousness in irony,

its grief in grace.
It invites you not to master it,
but to dance clumsily with it.
It doesn't ask for perfection —
only presence.
Only gratitude for the breath that quietly fills your lungs,
for the absurd beauty of each drama you create and
survive.

Be playful.
Be easy with yourself.
Laugh at the grand, imperfect design of it all.

Life is not a problem to solve —
it is a poem to live,
a mystery to savor,
a fleeting echo to be sung with joy.

Choose to live lightly,
yet walk with grace.
That is all life ever asked of you.

Love Forgives, Pride Remembers

When Love and Pride Spoke

Love:

He loves me truly.
I feel it — deep, humming through my bones.

Pride:

Then why, dear Love,
has he never introduced you to his world?
Are you a secret he holds
or a treasure he hides?

Love:

When he looks into my eyes,
when he holds me —
it heals something ancient inside me.

Pride:

And yet,

when you speak of marriage,
he looks away —
and the old ache of abandonment returns,
doesn't it?

Love:
He feels everything —
wildly, wholly,
his heart beats with furious tenderness.

Pride:
Yet how lightly he lets you carry the weight,
how little he tries
to truly understand.

Love:
Had we met at the right time,
he would have shouted my name to the stars,
claimed me without hesitation.

Pride:
But, dear Love,
the right soul doesn't ask for the right time.
They make it right — simply by choosing you.

Love:
Love asks for nothing in return.

It folds another life into its own —
gently, without counting.

I forgive him.

Pride:
And yet — he measures, he takes,
and forgets that giving, too,
is a language of love.

Love:
Let the war within me end.

Pride:
Let her rise —
beautiful, unshaken,
a blessing in every life she touches.

(Together, softly:)
Love wins.
Pride cheers.

Warrior in Silence

You see through people with piercing grace,
Yet lend a hand, even in the cruelest place.
You sleep alone, rise with no one near,
Still mend the wounds of others, hold their pain dear.

The mother who was meant to be your guide,
Left when you needed her at your side.
Still, in silence, you send her care—
A whispered prayer hangs in the air.

A father, your pillar, crumbled with ease,
Left you stranded, no moment of peace.
Your sibling stood with them, blind to the cost,
Yet your heart forgives, though deeply lost.

You're more than a survivor of days turned cold—
A wonder, a warrior, a soul made of gold.
You gather your wins with quiet grace,
Fighting each day with a brave, bright face.

You dream of being a husband, steady and true,
Yet miss the friend who shows up in all you do.
You wonder if you'll make a parent wise,
Yet guide with a coach's heart and quiet eyes.
You pray for a sign, a soul set free,
Yet overlook the light you've come to be.
You are winning in ways the world has yet to see.

Echoes of the Brave

If courage is missing,
intent holds no weight,
words fall empty,
and actions come late.

You speak of vision,
you dream of change,
but without bold steps,
it's all just arranged.

Prove not with speeches,
nor with grand show,
for truth lives in motion,
in the path you go.

Build up the courage,
let silence be loud,
your quiet conviction
will humble the proud.

And if you should stumble,
or fall on the way,
you'll still earn honor
for trying to stay.

For failure with heart
beats silence with pride—
when you've dared to act,
there's nothing to hide.

Grace in the Grind

You put your body through agony, shred each muscle,
Sweat every drop until your soul starts to hustle—
All to release joy wrapped in a chemical haze,
Pain becomes the price for those lighter days.

You tear yourself open to bring life anew,
Endure heartbreak, shame, and guilt, too.
From ruins and wreckage, resilience is born,
A silent warrior, shaped and worn.

You kneel in sorrow, plead for a sign,
Only to rise—healed, and divine.
A healer to many, once lost and torn,
From the ache of prayers, wisdom is born.

You argue, withdraw, feel deeply unheard,
Only to learn that love speaks beyond words.
In breaking, you uncover what matters the most,
A bond worth mending, a heart worth its post.

You nod through conflict, swallow your voice,
Trade peace for silence, and call it choice.
Yet somehow that quiet leads to the climb—
You call it success, the cost is time.

Life thrives in this curious crossroad of pain,
A simple paradox with truths to explain.
You cannot just survive—you must dive,
Into stillness, into scars—**to truly thrive**.

The Moment Gods Turn Away

The whispers in my ear ignite
a wildfire of wildest dreams,
before reality arrives,
a warm kiss lands on my neck—
tranquil, soft—
more potent than sleep.
No wine, no smoke, no drug
could mimic this high.
Your touch—
a charged spell of electricity—
makes me forget to breathe,
and shy away from myself.
The world falls mute.
Chaos hushes.
Your kiss—deep, wet, warm—
like sweet poison,
steals my senses,
leaving behind
only craving.

My fingers weave through wild hair,
yearning to be held,
as breath grows heavy—
deeper,
like drowning willingly
just to feel this alive.
My heart pounds louder
than reason,
but let this moment stretch,
even if gods
turn away, embarrassed
by the beauty
of souls intertwined.
Two pulses,
one rhythm.
One touch,
infinite echoes.
A love not just felt—
but lived,
breathed,
forever.

Hold My Hands, Mom

Hold my hands, Mom —
my shelter in chaos,
my calm in the storm.

In a world that surprises,
tests, and sometimes breaks me,
I walk forward with courage,
because I know —
your hands are always there.

I fall.
I bruise.
I chase wild dreams
and stumble through fears.
But I rise —
because I know you're near,
quietly holding space,
holding my hands.

Words aren't always needed.

A sigh is enough
for you to worry,
to understand,
to hold my hands
before I even reach out.

You are my quiet strength,
my unspoken comfort —
a love I never question,
a bond I never doubt.

But there will be moments
when I won't hold your hands —
not because I'm drifting,
but because I need to stand
on my own trembling feet.

I may not ask for help
or lean in every time.
That's not distance —
that's growth.
So hold my hands,
not to shield me,
but to stand beside me
as I learn.

Hold my hands

when I feel lost,
but let me wander
long enough to find myself.

Hold my hands
when others enter my life —
not in comparison,
but in celebration
of the love you taught me to give.

I will always come back —
not out of need,
but out of love.
You were my first warmth,
my first guide,
my forever place to land.

Hold my hands, Mom —
not because I'm fragile,
but because you're home.

The Quiet That Knows Me

The world around me buzzes —
rushing, relentless,
pausing for no one.
My mind, a flood
of thoughts, beliefs, dreams,
fears and dread —
an unending tide
that stops for no one.

My heart —
brimming with joy and despair,
carrying hopes, heartbreaks,
and quiet betrayals —
beats on, unyielding,
and stops for no one.

My body aches,
swells with time,
wears the weight of my lineage —
every scar, every curve,

a silent echo of those before me —
and still, it stops for no one.

But the moment I sit,
eyes closed,
and breathe...
just breathe —
the chaos softens.
The noise dissolves.
Time exhales.

Who do I owe this stillness to?
My Guru —
whose grace cracked me open.
My pain —
that became the path.
My longing —
for truth, for home.

With every breath,
I drift into a quiet abyss,
peaceful and magnetic —
a place I never wish to leave.
With every breath,
a calm washes over me,
like I'm floating on an unseen ocean,
gazing skyward,

as the sky lovingly gazes back.

With every breath,
a whisper, a secret,
like God tracing wisdom in my ears.

And with every breath,
I pray —
that one day,
in this stillness,
in this grace,
in this breath,
I'll pass quietly —
liberated,
whole,
free —
held in the arms of my Guru.

Unspoken, Unbroken

"It's Always His Eyes," she said—
Calm, sharp, and quietly magnetic,
The kind that make her want to shed every boundary
She built to feel safe.

"It's her smile," he whispered—
Seductive, yet laced with warmth,
A curve that could lead him anywhere,
Even to the ends of himself.

He is a child at heart,
Afraid of emotions, terrified of criticism—
She watches him with a tenderness
Only love can shape.

She is a soul stitched together
From too many breakages,
A warrior cloaked in grace—
And he worries, reverently.

He speaks little, acts even less,
But she knows—his silence is full of love.
She, on the other hand,
Loves like fire and fights like one,
But her heart always lands in the right place.

They both look up at the sky,
As if God might finally answer—
Hearts heavy with the weight of distance,
Egos unshed, forgiveness withheld.

Yet somewhere deep inside,
A flame refuses to die—
A dream, a desire,
A hope that love,
Even complicated love,
Might still find its way home.

In My Head, You Know Me

I've loved you in a million ways,
from stages I'll never stand on,
to dreams spun in the quiet corners
of rooms where your voice plays on loop.

You don't know I exist—
and yet, I've memorized the curve of your smile,
the way your eyes hold galaxies,
the grace with which you break the world and heal it
again with a lyric.
Is it foolish?

To feel this pulse of love so strong,
when logic whispers, *it's just in your head*?
But isn't that where all love begins—
in a single thought,
a heartbeat,
a longing?

You are not mine,
yet you've taught me to feel deeply,
to imagine fiercely,
to adore selflessly,
with no demand but the joy of loving.

And if I can offer such boundless affection
to someone who doesn't even see me—
why not to those around me?
Why not to the friend who checks in,
the stranger who smiles,
the soul beside me who aches to be seen?

Perhaps love isn't about being returned,
but about being awakened.
And you, in your unknowable beauty,
have awakened the lover in me.

Rational Lies

He left his newborn, never looked back—
said nothing, just vanished.
They said he had his reasons.

The doctor let her slip away,
too much pain to bear, they said.
He had his reasons.

She strayed and stayed silent,
a secret buried in kisses and tears—
she had her reasons.

They ended a boy,
young, loud, innocent.
They, too, had their reasons.

She walked away from her home,
from blood, from name—
to serve a God none had seen.
She had her reasons.

They broke his heart,
to build him a better life,
or so they said.
Parents have their reasons.

They kill, conquer, crucify—
for flags, for faith, for land.
Each reason sharper than the last.

The child cries through the night,
no sleep, no peace—
but the little one, too,
has his reasons.

And in this world,
where every wound is stitched with excuses,
every sin cloaked in logic,
every truth twisted by peace—
what's left of right and wrong?

We wear our reasons like armor,
lie loud enough to believe ourselves.
Fairness is a fairytale.
We are beasts,
but well-spoken ones.

Too Much or Never Enough

I love with a heart wide open,
pure as a mother's first touch—
yet you leave,
without a goodbye, without a flinch.

I'm left clutching the silence,
wondering if I was foolish
to trust so easily,
to love so deeply,
to give without keeping score.

You break more than my heart—
you shatter my faith,
my ability to believe
that love won't always leave.

Am I unworthy?
A red flag dressed in warmth?
I search for flaws in my reflection,
blame the softness in my soul.

I was the giver,
the quiet dreamer,
asking for nothing
but hoping for everything.

Yet you walked away,
like I was air—
felt but never seen,
known but never kept.

Was I too easy to walk over,
or was I never meant to be cherished?
Did even the One who made me
decide I was too much,
or worse—
not enough?

What did I do
to burn so bright
that you felt the need to run?
Or was that your plan all along—
and I just couldn't see it?

"Why me?" I scream into the silence,
while God waits,
not to punish,

but to answer—
only when I'm quiet enough
to finally listen.

Darkness With Morals

You can throw your words like daggers,
or choose silence like a coward's sword —
but this spirit?
Too dark to beg. Too wild to bend.

You say you want me,
but fear the fire that shaped me.
Not all souls come soft and sweet —
some are steel,
tempered by betrayal,
rebuilt in the ashes of too many goodbyes.

You look for light,
but flinch at my shadow.
You seek sweetness,
but gag at the taste of my truth.

I've outgrown your approval.
I'm bulletproof —
to your love,

to your hate,
to your confusion wrapped in charm.

I don't pick battles,
but I never walk away from them.
I don't harm —
unless harm knocks first.

There's no halo above this head,
just darkness with a code,
with teeth,
with pride.

And no —
I'm not sorry.
Not even a little.

The House That Memory Built

They seem joint at the hip —
laughing loud at old tales,
but truly, just distant cousins
raised under one roof of fading paint and fragile ties.

Childhood binds them,
not trust.
Memories stitch their bond,
while resentments simmer below stitched smiles.

Some scrape by for a living,
some scrape together broken pride.
Some chase connection,
others master the art of hide and seek —
hiding pain, hiding truth, hiding who they've become.

They quarrel like warriors mid-battle,
then patch up
like nothing was ever broken —

but it always is,
just not enough to admit.

They call each other siblings,
but celebrate in secret
when one stumbles —
a twisted comfort in someone else's fall.

Well-wishers by name,
but their hearts flinch
when one dares to rise too high,
too free,
too far.

Love exists —
but only in the shadows of shared misery.
Not trust, no —
just pride in the blood
and blind allegiance to a name.

Too foolish to hate,
too bound to leave,
too real to romanticize.

They're chaos.
They're contradiction.
They're mine.

My loving, crazy bloodline.

Blood That Remembers

We share no cradle, no surname, no home,
Yet the pain we carry feels eerily known.
Bruised not by each other,
But by ghosts who called themselves father and mother.

You flinch at anger, I shrink at pride,
Two different pasts where innocence died.
Your silence comes from battles never fought,
Mine from wars that were waged in thought.

We walk with shadows stitched in our spine,
The shame, the secrets, the untold line.
Their choices, their chaos, their cowardly ways—
We bleed in present from their yesterdays.

But we—
We are not them.

You mend with tears, I mend with fire,
Both burning down the funeral pyre.

Not of bodies, but beliefs,
Of love twisted and griefs bequeathed.

We vow not vengeance, but a vow so rare—
That our children breathe unburdened air.
No hand-me-down guilt, no silence to keep,
No nightmares disguised in lullabies deep.

We'll name the wounds, and let them fade,
Not hide them beneath the beds we made.
We won't be perfect, but we'll be clean,
Free of the curse passed in our genes.

Two branches born of poisoned roots,
Daring to bloom with gentler fruits.

The chain ends here—this is our stand,
We may be bruised, but we are the healing hand.

If She Calls, I'll Bury the Body

She didn't come from my womb,
Yet, she feels like a missing twin—
Born late, but born just right,
To be the spark in my shadows, the calm in my fight.

She's teenage thunder wrapped in grace,
Fire in her soul, mischief on her face.
Rules are suggestions, norms—mere games,
And when the world gets loud, she calls my name.

She tells me her heartbreaks in unfiltered truths,
Like poetry spoken in messy youth.
No drama, no flair—just raw, uncut,
The kind of honesty that leaves you gut-punched and
healed in one breath.

Once, I cried behind closed doors,
And she, a toddler, crawled in with toys and giggles
galore.

She didn't fix my world—but she made me play,
And in that innocent act, she chased the pain away.

Now, she speaks wisdom in teenage slang,
A prophet disguised in Vans and tangled bangs.
I listen, and I learn.
I teach, and she burns—bright, curious, fierce.

She says if she kills, I'll bury the body.
She's not wrong. I'd go without blinking.
I say if I fall, she'll catch me laughing,
With glitter on her face and chaos in her thinking.
We aren't just blood—we are chosen, aligned.

A secret language, a pact undefined.
She is my number one fan, my tiny mirror,
And I, her lifelong guardian, louder cheerer.
If soul sisters exist across time and space,

Then we must have once shared a womb or a place.
Maybe we were stars beside each other once—
Promising to find again in life's next dance.

So here we are—
One growing wild, one holding space.
Two rebels in sync, in different life pace.
She pledges to love me with reckless might,

And I vow to guard her day and night.

She, my compass when I feel hollow—
Me, her anchor, when storms start to follow.

Together, we write a story rare and true—
Of loyalty, laughter, and a love that grew.

Gods in Disguise

They stand as silent sentinels,
Behind the sacred walls, where peace dwells.
With hearts unburdened, minds so clear,
They greet each soul, embracing fear.

I wander in, a stranger unknown,
With a restless heart, a seed unshone.
But they, they see something divine—
As if my presence, a spark to align.

I ask, how do they give so much,
Their hands, their hearts, their every touch—
Without a thought of what's returned,
Without a single desire burned?

They offer their time, their energy, their grace,
To guide the lost, to help them embrace
The path unknown, the journey deep,
To hold their hand when doubts creep.

I, a mere traveler, stumble in the dark,
They shine their light, ignite a spark—
I wonder, in their quiet dedication,
What strength lies beneath their silent foundation?

With every smile, they heal, they serve,
Without a thought, without a curve
Of expectation, not a trace,
Of wanting more from this sacred space.

They are the limbs of the Guru's grace,
In their eyes, a calm embrace.
They are Gods in human form—
Willing to weather every storm.

To dedicate your life to this path,
Without a second thought, without the wrath—
To serve with love, with heart so pure,
Is a strength I long to endure.

For in their humble act of service,
Lies the secret to life's true purpose.
They are the silent pillars of light,
Making the world a little more right.

So here's to them, my silent guides,
Who stand with grace by Guru's side,

May we all learn, in time, to be—
A reflection of their love, so free.

48

Fear's Favorite Muse

If Fear were a person,
she'd whisper gently in my ear at night,
not to scare me —
but to remind me of everything I might lose.
She'd sit beside me during my biggest wins,
clutching my hand,
just in case it all falls apart tomorrow.

She'd dress in shadows,
not to hide herself,
but to make sure I noticed
every uncertain flicker of light.

And beside her,
always humming and skipping,
was her best friend —
Dream.
The bold one.
The beautiful fool.
The one who dared to reach

where Fear only watched.

Dream would build castles out of clouds,
while Fear pointed out
how easily they could crumble.
But somehow,
Dream never stopped building.
They fought often —
Fear throwing anchors,
Dream spreading wings.

But they always came back to each other.
Because Fear kept Dream grounded,
and Dream gave Fear a purpose.
I live with them both,
these strange companions.

One teaches caution,
the other, courage.
And in the dance between doubt and desire,
I learn what it means to be alive.